Fall

OUR FOUR SEASONS

Aaron Carr and Heather Kissock

LIGHTB◆X
openlightbox.com

LIGHTBOX

Go to
www.openlightbox.com,
and enter this book's
unique code.

ACCESS CODE

LBJ78993

Lightbox is an all-inclusive digital solution for the teaching and learning of curriculum topics in an original, groundbreaking way. Lightbox is based on National Curriculum Standards.

OPTIMIZED FOR

✓ **TABLETS**
✓ **WHITEBOARDS**
✓ **COMPUTERS**
✓ **AND MUCH MORE!**

STANDARD FEATURES OF LIGHTBOX

AUDIO High-quality narration using text-to-speech system

VIDEOS Embedded high-definition video clips

ACTIVITIES Printable PDFs that can be emailed and graded

WEBLINKS Curated links to external, child-safe resources

SLIDESHOWS Pictorial overviews of key concepts

INTERACTIVE MAPS Interactive maps and aerial satellite imagery

QUIZZES Ten multiple choice questions that are automatically graded and emailed for teacher assessment

KEY WORDS Matching key concepts to their definitions

VIDEOS

WEBLINKS

SLIDESHOWS

QUIZZES

2

Fall

OUR FOUR SEASONS

In this book, you will learn

what it is

when it is

what happens

what we do

and much more!

3

A year is made up of four seasons.

Fall is one of the seasons.

It comes after summer and before winter.

September 22

Fall starts on September 22 or September 23.

5

Fall is a time of change.

Days become shorter.

Nights become longer.

Some places in Alaska can have nights that last two months in the fall.

The weather begins to cool once fall starts.

Fall brings rain.

It may even snow.

Trees change color in the fall.

Green leaves turn yellow, brown, orange, or red.

They then fall from the tree.

Animals start to get ready
for winter.

Some grow thick fur
to stay warm.

Others change color
to help them hide in the snow.

Some animals move
to a new home in the fall.

Many birds fly to warmer places.

Other animals look for a place
to sleep.

A gray whale may swim more than 6,000 miles in the fall to find warm waters.

People get ready
for winter as well.

They clean their yards.

They rake their leaves.

17

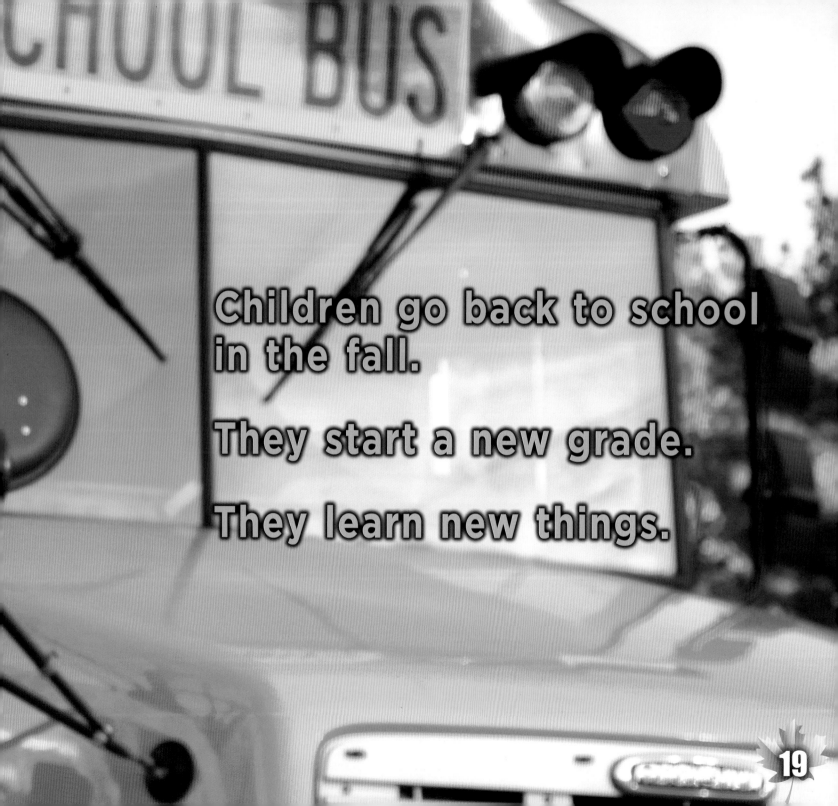

Children go back to school in the fall.

They start a new grade.

They learn new things.

Farmers pick their fruits and vegetables in the fall.

This is called the harvest.

The Moon may look large and red in the fall. This is called a harvest moon.

Fall Quiz

Fall is all about changes. What changes do you see in these pictures?

KEY WORDS

Research has shown that as much as 65 percent of all written material published in English is made up of 300 words. These 300 words cannot be taught using pictures or learned by sounding them out. They must be recognized by sight. This book contains 69 common sight words to help young readers improve their reading fluency and comprehension. This book also teaches young readers several important content words, such as proper nouns. These words are paired with pictures to aid in learning and improve understanding.

Page	Sight Words First Appearance
4	a, four, is, made, of, up, year
5	after, and, before, comes, it, on, one, or, starts, the
6	change, days, nights, time
7	can, have, in, last, places, some, that, two
8	begins, even, may, once, to
10	from, leaves, then, they, trees, turn
12	animals, for, get, grow, help, others, them
14	home, look, many, move, new
15	find, miles, more, than, waters
17	as, people, their, well
19	back, children, go, learn, school, things
20	this
21	large

Page	Content Words First Appearance
4	seasons
5	fall, summer, winter
7	Alaska, months
8	rain, weather
10	color
12	fur, snow
14	birds
15	gray whale
17	yards
19	grade
20	farmers, fruits, harvest, vegetables
21	Moon

Published by Smartbook Media Inc.
350 5th Avenue, 59th Floor New York, NY 10118
Website: www.openlightbox.com

Library of Congress Control Number: 2015942226

ISBN 978-1-5105-0166-9 (hardcover)
ISBN 978-1-5105-0167-6 (multi-user ebook)

Printed in Guangzhou, China
3 4 5 6 7 8 9 0 23 22 21 20 19

082019
190826

Editor: Heather Kissock
Art Director: Terry Paulhus

Every reasonable effort has been made to trace ownership and to obtain permission to reprint copyright material. The publisher would be pleased to have any errors or omissions brought to its attention so that they may be corrected in subsequent printings.

The publisher acknowledges iStock as its primary image supplier for this title.